1

Think Like Socrates

Unlock the Power of Socratic Questioning to Improve Your Critical Thinking and Persuasion Skills.

By Steven Schuster

www.stevenschusterbooks.com

contained herein may not be suitable for everyone. This work is sold with the understanding that the author is not engaged in rendering medical, legal or other professional advice or services. If professional assistance is required, the services of a competent professional person should be sought. The author shall not be liable for damages arising herefrom. The fact that an individual, organization of website is referred to in this work as a citation and/or potential source of further information does not mean that the author endorses the information the individual, organization to the website may provide or recommendations they/it may make. Further, readers should be aware that Internet websites listed in this work might have changed or disappeared between when this work was written and when it is read.

For general information on the products and services or to obtain technical support, please contact the author.

Visit www.stevenschusterbooks.com to download your FREE EBOOK, The Misguided Mind! Get fascinated by the depth of our own cognitive biases!

Does your impulsive thinking bring only trouble? Do you often grab your head muttering "what was I thinking?" Would you like to understand your brain's inner workings better?

This little free eBook will give you a crash course in *the most common cognitive biases*. These ingrained thought patterns come to us naturally, thus we don't think that we think in a distorted way. However, they can have severe negative effect on our lives. Knowing what they are and how to identify them, we can help ourselves making better choices. Learn:
 •Why are first impressions so powerful and permanent?
 •Why do we rely on the first thought that pops into our mind?
 •How can certain advertisements make us open our wallet immediately?
 •How and why does our memory fool us daily?

Visit www.stevenschusterbooks.com to download your FREE EBOOK, The Misguided Mind! Get fascinated by the depth of our own cognitive biases!

Table of Contents

Introduction

Greetings! My name is Socrates, and my thoughts changed the world. But that's a bold and conceited statement for an introduction, so allow me to tell you a more detailed version of my story. As we speak, I'm sitting in a jail cell on the outskirts of Athens. Within minutes, a guard will bring me a drink. It will be a cup of hemlock, a poisonous potion prompting a paralytic passing. I shall empty the cup following which act I will become very sleepy and shut my eyes forever soon afterward. But before that happens, I wanted to share some of my ideas with you.

I was born in Athens in ancient Greece. Always a private person, wishing to keep this habit in my last moments, too. Without too many personal details, I'm comfortable confessing that I have the reputation of a mysterious troublemaker in my homeland. People call me the first Western philosopher, but I don't indulge in such self-polishing thoughts. Philosophers usually flatter themselves thinking they know a lot about the world. I don't think I know that much.

The Peloponnesian war left a mark on my mind, and after returning to Athens, I isolated myself to think a bit. In my time, wisdom was the coolest label you could possess. If someone gathered a large support group behind his ideas, he was proclaimed wise. I took such "wisdom" with a large grain of salt. In my experience, many people who seem to be or claim to be wise are not that wise. This naturally proposes a problem. Those who believe in the authority of this sage, will blindly follow him, often at the cost of severe consequences.

Questioning wisdom helps you discover flaws in it. If you don't question, knowledge stands still as a rock instead of flowing and carving new ground like a river. Following this realization, I started asking questions more intentionally.

I discovered that questioning a claim of something being true, tests its validity. If you question someone and they can prove that their claim is legit, great job. You made sure you're not signing up for spreading false information, and you also helped someone practice defending their truth.

For example, if someone claims that it is essential to worship the god Ares, I would ask, "What is essentialism? What is worshipping? Are there other gods to worship?" If they can't articulate essentialism, how can they claim it is essential to worship Ares? If they can't explain what worship is, how can they know if they are worshipping Ares, and therefore that they are doing an essential act?

If someone making claims can't answer the challenges imposed by questioning, how can they state that their claim is true?

Plato, a bright young man used to follow me around Athens, learning my questioning style which he eventually bestowed upon his student – Aristotle. He became the teacher of Alexander the Great. Alexander spread these teachings in his large kingdom. Eventually, the Romans occupying Alexander's empire helped spread this questioning tradition further. After the Roman Empire fell apart, this precious knowledge rested idle for centuries until the miracle of the Renaissance happened. People again read the works of Plato and Aristotle and re-discovered the power of methodical questioning, and testing of claims – the style you today know as Socratic Questioning. I feel honored by the label.

Questioning gets a bad reputation. Some mistakenly think that asking a question or many questions, means that the question maker is uneducated, or unwise. I think the opposite.

True wisdom lies in the knowledge of acknowledging how little we actually know.

When one gets to this realization, they can ask questions and get to more accurate facts. This being said, I must warn you that asking questions – and people being unable to answer them - can also be a quick way to make people resentful.

I'm guilty of embarrassing a handful of important men in Athens who took my questions personally. When my questions highlighted their ignorance, they took it even worse. These VIPs -as you'd call them today - saw that others asked question like I did, so

I was arrested for corrupting the fine people of Athens. Plato wrote a noteworthy piece about my trial and how I fought to defend myself utilizing the same questioning style for which I was arrested. Needless to say, that this made my enemies even more bitter.

I was convicted. The court mistakenly asked me what I believed my punishment should be. I answered that they should feed me with a tasty meal every night at the sacred heart of the city to honor my achievement of opening the eyes of the people of Athens to real wisdom. My enemies did not appreciate neither my wit nor my suggestion. They assessed that my insolence is beyond redemption so they sentenced me to death.

I haven't got much time left so I'll leave you with this: remember, the only thing you know for certain is that you know nothing. But don't take my word for it for I know nothing.

Chapter 1. A Man of Mystery

Socrates was a man shrouded in mystery. He bucked the typical Athenian standards of his time (c. 470-399 BCE), yet what little we know about him comes from secondhand sources with questionable reliability. [i]

For one of the world's most well-known philosophers, Socrates wrote nothing himself, but over the passing centuries, has almost become a character with different personality traits depending on the era the author was writing in or their beliefs.[ii]

Much of what has been written about Socrates has been rejected as false. Referring to historical sources rather than more modern versions, which have taken certain liberties, we learned that Socrates stood out among his contemporaries in Athens. In an age where good looks and maintaining a healthy body were directly tied to success, the historical sources all readily agree that Socrates was unattractive in every way, including looking as if he'd skipped many meals rather than having the preferred aesthetic of a "potbelly." Historical accounts and drawings and busts from this period look nothing like the later statues depicting Socrates with a more handsome visage. We commonly see these later images on websites and dust jackets today.[iii]

Beyond being recognizable for his notoriously bad appearance, Socrates was also a well-known and controversial person in

Athens to the point he was mocked in plays by other philosophers of the era. He was often the butt of jokes in plays, subject to much comic ridicule. Aristophanes' *The Clouds* is a perfect example of this. In his play, Aristophanes uses Socrates as the main character to show immorality and atheism immediately following the deeper examination of language and nature, none of which accurately portrays philosophical study.[iv]

However, Socrates had his supporters, but much of their work wasn't performed until after his death. For example, Plato's *Apology of Socrates* is allegedly the defense given by Socrates at his trial when he was charged for irreverence toward the gods of Athens.[v] In this "apology," Plato depicts Socrates as a man of integrity, intellect, and self-control, who possessed exceptional skills to frame an argument for discussion or debate. Despite their significant age difference—Plato was an infant when *The Clouds* was written in circa 423 BCE—the relationship between Plato and Socrates was that of a mentor/mentee.[vi]

Aristotle's work also provided us with insight into Socrates' personality. In 367 BCE, Aristotle attended Academy, a school owned by Plato. Because we know Socrates and Plato had such a close relationship, it is unlikely Socrates' methods and ideas would not have been discussed in the school. In later writings about Socrates, Aristotle says that Socrates asked questions, but he declined to give answers, and that was because he lacked the knowledge to do so. Aristotle further said Socrates looked to define the virtues, but that he did not spend his time studying nature, but rather ethics.[vii]

In the years leading to Socrates' trial and subsequent death, the military force had been fighting against Sparta for thirty years due to the Peloponnesian War. This had granted Athenian citizens significant freedom, given they didn't disrupt the democracy or break the law. However, in 399 BCE, Socrates was charged with irreverence toward the gods. In the years during and immediately following the Peloponnesian War, there were several attempts to overthrow the democracy of Athens and religious scandals that had primed both the public and officials. After the previous events, there was a definite expectation that future perpetrators would be brought up on charges.[viii]

The mood of the Athenians was further soured as they particularly did not like Socrates. This was expressed in Plato's *Apology of Socrates.* In *Apology,* we saw Socrates as someone who repeatedly tried to do his best by his community. But no matter what he did, they were unimpressed and hostile. Socrates was not a wealthy man and lacked political influence. He knew he would be found guilty and face death despite his desire and genuine attempts to help the people of Athens.[ix] Socrates was found guilty of impiety and sentenced to death for his crimes.[x]

The death of Socrates was almost as famous as his life and teachings. Many people can immediately tell you how Socrates died—he committed suicide by drinking a cup of poison hemlock. Socrates did this because that is how Athenians carried out death sentences at the time. He was made to become his own executioner. Socrates had earnestly tried to win his trial, but his attitude and previous history worked against him.

While we know how Socrates died, we know close to nothing about how he was as a child. Can you imagine how often he must have asked *"why"* from his parents? It's almost scary to picture a Socrates-level childlike curiosity. We can assume that the philosopher was inquisitive from an early age, sharpening his intellect and ability to question. How did he develop his methodical questioning style? Was it something that he intentionally prepared for? Or was it rather the result of repetition? What do you think?

We rely significantly on others and their impressions of Socrates to form our assessment of the controversial philosopher's ideas, thoughts, and assessments. This makes Socrates and his philosophy something of a mystery. This book aims to unveil the secrets and introduce you to his techniques and how to use them in your everyday life.

The birth of Socratic Questioning.

Chaerophon, one of Socrates' close friends, visited the Oracle of Delphi, the most important and respected shrine in Greece, and asked if there was a wiser man than Socrates.[xi] The Oracle claimed that Socrates was the wisest man in Greece. When Socrates heard what the Oracle had said, he was surprised. The Oracle would have to be wiser than Socrates to know exactly how wise Socrates was and name him the wisest man in Greece. This was the fateful beginning of Socratic questioning.

Firm in his resolution, Socrates attempted to find a wiser man than himself. He sought and asked questions from fellow Athenians known to be sagacious. The mere fact that he questioned the Oracle of Delphi's judgment was an outrageous deed. Plus, all the insolent questions he peppered the good sages of Athens in his attempt to find *the truth*.

Finding the truth is at the heart of Socratic questioning. By asking meaningful questions, we expand our knowledge as we hear out the arguments of others. [xii] The Socratic method is not a debate, and the individuals participating in the process are not there to defend their viewpoint. The participants are present because they want to work together to discover the truth. But this is a tricky undertaking as what's true to one person might not be true for another.

Socrates noticed that different words and expressions meant different things to different people. Thus, in his quest to find the truth, he established that one must define a concept well. Now, finding a perfect definition is not an easy task.

Let's try to define what justice is. The definition of it? People have different opinions on how to define justice depending on their worldview and the values and norms created by their families and society. Some people will see justice as a black-and-white issue, a set of rules that should never be broken. Others will consider the issue's circumstances as mitigating factors, meaning justice can be more of a gray area. And some would state, "justice is when you get what you deserve." But who is the judge of what one deserves?

In the following example, let's assume that following the law is the definition of justice.

Jack works in a supermarket and spots a customer attempting to steal items. He reports this to the manager on duty, who promptly calls the police. The police arrive at the store, and the woman is about to be arrested when Jack overhears the customer apologizing to the store manager as she explains she can't feed her children right now as she had recently lost her job. In a show of sympathy for the woman's plight, the manager decides not to press charges against her.

In this scenario, Jack might use Socratic questioning to ask, "If we don't follow through with prosecuting this woman, as awful as her situation is, will others believe they can steal from us too?" "Has the woman attempted to use one of the foodbanks in the area, and what other resources can we direct her to?" "How do shoplifters affect our livelihood? If our store experiences too much shoplifting, we would go out of business."

Sticking to the belief that "following the law is justice," these are valid questions when thinking about handling such a difficult predicament. By employing these questions, the idea is to see the bigger picture. Using the

Socratic method on our day-to-day moral dilemmas can help us find our true sense of justice to wrap our heads around some difficult situations. What would you have done? What would your belief about justice be?

As we saw, it was difficult to pinpoint an accurate and universal definition for the concept of justice. Socrates realized this, too. So, he was set in developing a way that gave birth to more precise definitions. He asked questions that got him closer to these definitions, sometimes to the embarrassment of others.

One of the primary tenets of the American justice system is that it is better to let ten guilty men go free than to allow one innocent man be convicted. However, today you can find countless cases that document police corruption and coercion against innocent men and women for the sake of closing a case, revenge, laziness, railroading, or money. These infamous cases include the Central Park 5, the Kids for Cash scandal in Luzerne County Court of Common Pleas in Wilkes-Barre, PA, and Nick Yarris. However, one prominent example of justice gone wrong is with American serial killer Kenneth McDuff.[xiii]

McDuff, also known as the Broomstick Killer, had the distinction of being one of twenty death row inmates but was paroled after his sentence was commuted. McDuff was originally convicted in 1966 and sentenced to death for murdering three teens with a broomstick. However, his sentence was commuted to life in 1972 when the Supreme Court of the United States declared the death penalty to be unconstitutional, and he was released on parole in 1989. McDuff was known to have killed again within three days of his release, and though he was sentenced to death again in 1993 for the murder of six additional women, he is alleged to have more victims who remain unidentified.

Many people were outraged when McDuff was identified as the killer in the subsequent six murders as they felt he should never have been released from prison. Texas citizens wanted to know if the original three victims had received justice as McDuff's original death sentence had not been carried out. The families and friends of the six new victims were outraged and asked why the Bureau of Prisons had approved parole for such a vicious murderer when had they not, it would have prevented McDuff from killing again.[xiv] What are your thoughts? Was justice served when McDuff was first sentenced? Was it justice to alleviate his punishment from death row to a life sentence? What about him being released on parole after serving 23 years in prison?

On knowledge

One thing is clear, focusing on finding a correct definition of concepts was critical to Socrates. He spent "most of its time defining just one term, justice." Plato wrote this in his work, the Republic, which contains the – probably - most well-known Socratic dialogue.[xv] Socrates argued that a man should actively seek knowledge to help him moderate his actions and thoughts. The best way to knowledge is by asking multiple sources, visiting the issue from various angles, and logically assessing information. In Socrates' mind, this was the way to wisdom.[xvi]

How would you define a car? Would it be something that people drive to get from A to B? Some may say they drive trucks, SUVs, boats, motorcycles, or mopeds. Almost any motorized vehicle that exists today can be driven, and they are all different. Cars can be electric, gasoline, or hybrid models. There are self-driving models to consider, and many people will even say the word "car" to be universally interchangeable with some of the other terms listed above, as that is used for their everyday transportation. When you stop and think about all these little details, Plato's demand for the perfect definition becomes quite the challenge.

The crucial part of the Socratic method is it allows us to ask the same questions repeatedly to define all the challenging questions we face throughout our lifetime. There is no requirement that we reach particular developmental milestones before employing Socratic questioning. We can use Socratic questioning on the same topic multiple times as we grow and change throughout our development as social, ethical, and physical beings.

Social scientists such as Art Chickering, Lawrence Kohlberg, and Erik Erikson built their careers and conducted extensive research on identity development. This research tells us that individuals move through specific stages or can even exist in multiple stages of development depending on several factors. As a person moves in and out of these developmental stages, their use of Socratic questioning would have them asking deeper, more profound questions and even changing their stances on some issues.[xvii]

When considering how this might look with other theoretical examples, we can look at Kohlberg's moral identity development. In a scenario of going to a homeless shelter and helping feed the homeless, someone in the early stages of developing their moral identity might employ questions such as, "How does helping the homeless benefit me? If I help the homeless, will the homeless be able to help me achieve something I need in return?" But a person in the later stages of developing their moral identity would ask, "Are there additional things I can do to help the homeless in my city? What do the homeless need to help them live stable and safe lives?" The more we grow, the more we know, we could conclude. But is that necessarily true?

Socrates found a definition of knowledge. He called it the absolute truth. He believed that everything in the universe was interconnected. Knowing one thing can help us derive potentially everything from that one central truth. Socrates intended to uncover basic ideas that he called forms. We can see this in action when Socrates asks Meno what virtue is.

Not grasping Socrates' intent, Meno gives examples of virtuous acts as his answer. This disappoints Socrates and informs him that he needs to tweak his question. Next time he asks Meno what those virtuous acts have in common. In Socrates' belief, whatever connects all virtuous acts is what virtue inherently is. If we think about a forest, a person can see the trees but not see the forest. The trees are the virtuous acts, and the forest is virtue itself. Once they understand what a forest or virtue is, they get a full grasp of the concept. Virtue is abstract; it exists outside the physical world, so unlike a visible-tangible forest, virtue is harder to fully get. The same goes for all forms of abstractions – they can't be grasped by the human senses, but they can be reasoned by human thought.[xviii]

What Socrates asks from Meno is not the dictionary-ready definition of virtue, more like the essence of virtue. This is an important distinction. A dictionary-ready or *nominal* definition describes something as precisely as possible, leaving no confusion about the described thing. We learn "how is this word used? Rather than "what this thing is?"[xix] A great definition must accomplish two things at once: on the one hand, it must be clear enough to be evident what we're talking about. But it should also leave no questions about how the described thing is distinct from all others. The definition of something thus has to be so descriptive and differentiating that we won't mistake it for another thing. The Socratic method helps pin down such definitions.

A polar bear is a big animal with white fur, right? But what is big exactly? That's a relative term. Big to you may not be big at all. And what about white rabbits, dogs, cats, and foxes? They all have white fur. There are also snow leopards and Siberian tigers. Aren't they also big animals with white fur? What sets polar bears apart from these other animals? These are the questions that should help one engage their critical thinking skills and provide a better definition of a polar bear. According to Socrates, we don't know the essence of a polar bear if we can't define it to exclude all other types of bears and other big animals with white fur.

Good definitions follow these six steps:

1. They are neither too narrow nor too broad.
2. They are clear, not vague.
3. They are literal, not figurative.
4. They are short, rather than long.
5. They are positive, instead of negative whenever possible.

6. They are to the point, not circular.[xx]

Socratic questioning, and its quest to find the truth in well-phrased definitions, resulted in the rise of two types of reasoning: deductive and inductive. If we utilize Socrates-approved definitions with these types of reasoning, and add some critical thinking, we practice something that's called the *scientific method*. Let's see the nominal definition and explanation for inductive and deductive reasoning.

Deductive reasoning begins with a general statement, (hypothesis) and examines the possibilities to reach a specific, logical conclusion.[xxi] It consists of a first premise, a second premise, and an inference (evidence and reasoning-based conclusion). For example,

44

Premise 1: All big cats have four legs.

Premise 2: Tigers are big cats.

Inference: Therefore, tigers have four legs.

Deductive reasoning must be sound. To achieve this, the hypothesis needs to be correct. We assume that premise 1, "All big cats have four legs" and premise 2, "tigers are big cats" are true. Thus, the inference is logical and also true. "In deductive reasoning, if something is true of a class of things in general, it is also true for all members of that class."[xxii]

Deductive reasoning is a solid thinking tool if the premises are true. But let's see a different example:

Premise 1: Grandmas make all homemade knitwear.

Premise 2: Anne knits for herself.

Inference: Therefore, Anne is a grandma.

As you can see, while this conclusion is valid in a logical sense, it's still untrue as premise 1 is false.

According to the University of Illinois in Springfield, inductive reasoning "involves finding the path that leads to a known solution. Inductive reasoning is the ability to combine information that may seem unrelated to form general rules or relationships. It is a primary attribute in scientific theory formulation. As an example of inductive reasoning, in a crime, you have the evidence. The goal is to use inductive reasoning to determine how the evidence came to be as it is."[xxiii]

In contrast with deductive reasoning, where we go from the general to the specific, we start at a specific point and go towards the general in inductive reasoning. "We make many observations, discern a pattern, make a generalization, and infer an explanation or a theory," Wassertheil-Smoller told Live Science. "In science, there is a constant interplay between inductive inference (based on observations) and deductive inference (based on theory), until we get closer and closer to the 'truth,' which we can only approach but not ascertain with complete certainty."[xxiv]

An example of inductive reasoning could be:

Premise 1: The ostrich is a bird.

Premise 2: The ostrich can't fly.

Inference A: Thus, birds can't fly.

Inference B: Thus, some birds can't fly.

Despite both premises being correct, ostriches are birds, and they can't fly, inductive reasoning can't guarantee that the conclusion will be correct. Inference A doesn't logically follow based on the premises. Inference B is probably true. After all, they are strong or weak with inductive conclusions, rather than valid or invalid.

Other examples of inductive reasoning could be:

Data: It rained a lot in the past five years.

Hypothesis: Probably it will rain a lot this year.

Data: I yawn whenever someone else yawns next to me.

Hypothesis: It's possible that yawning is contagious.

The goal of inductive reasoning is to find patterns and create rules to explain the observed phenomena.

Socratic questioning is a form of critical thinking.

When we use the Socratic Method to question things, to sharper our definitions to get to the truth of a matter, we practice *critical thinking.* To meaningfully question an argument, we first must understand that argument well. After we deepen our knowledge about the argument itself, we can look for weaknesses based on which we may ask our questions. Weaknesses usually present themselves in the form of assumptions. We can ask, "how do these assumptions prove or disprove the argument? What are the assumptions based on?"

How is the argument defined? What is clear, and what is distinct about it? What alternative viewpoints could this argument be presented from? Look for the answer to all these questions. Try to see the issue from different perspectives. This is how you practice Socratic questioning.

The steps of Socratic questioning

Beginning the process of Socratic Questioning can be overwhelming. Where do you start when presented with an argument? What do you question? How do you do it? Start by paraphrasing the argument and then summarize it. Whatever we understand, we can summarize. If you don't understand something, ask questions about those terms and phrases to gain clarity. Before you engage in asking questions, understand the argument perfectly. Otherwise, your questions will be weakly relevant.

1. Ask for an opinion or a definition. Formulate your question clearly and precisely. Keep an emotional distance from the matter. The more invested you are emotionally in a

subject, the harder it will be to stay impartial and logical.

2. Build on this initial opinion or definition by asking questions that offer further clarification, understanding, and precision.

3. Gather the relevant information from the answer to your question and assess it with logic.

4. If you need further clarification, ask follow-up questions. Approach the issue with open-mindedness and curiosity, with a thirst to learn.

5. Look for assumptions and biases in the answer but also in your questions.

6. Ask about the source of information. Do other sources support it? Can it be verified?

7. Don't jump to conclusions prematurely. When facing a complex issue, take time to think about both your questions and the answers. Analyze if logic holds in the context in which the answers are presented. Would a conclusion follow effortlessly, or would it be contrived?

8. Enjoy the collaboration of idea sharing as both you and the one you question will now have access to a better, deeper understanding of the questioned phenomenon.

9. This shall only work if both of you are invested in finding the truth instead of defending your viewpoint.

10. Accept that the Socratic questioning may cause dissatisfactory answers and results. This happens because the goal is not to convince but to learn.

Picture 1[xxv]: Socratic Questioning Map.

Consider the picture above. Its implicit classifications can help you better understand

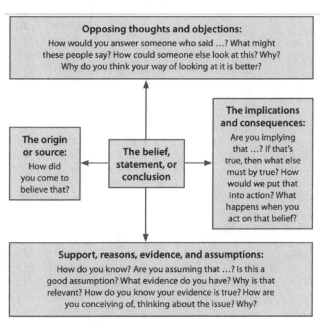

these important aspects of thinking in a Socratic fashion:

"All thinking has a history in the lives of particular persons.

All thinking depends upon a substructure of reasons, evidence, and assumptions.

All thinking leads us in some direction or other (has implications and

consequences).

All thinking stands in relation to other possible ways to think (there is never just one way to think about something)."[xxvi]

Taking all this into account, reflect on how you came to think the way you think about a certain issue. Why. List the reasons, assumptions, and sources that underlie what you think.

Approaches to Socratic Questioning

1. *The Boot Camp Approach.* This approach aims to break the person in the "boot camp." Imagine you are a brand new private in the army, and your boss is a big mean drill sergeant who has it out for you. In all your meetings, your boss drills you constantly, asking question after question until he finally asks one you don't have a response for. Thankfully, we don't see this high-pressure approach too much anymore, which is likely better for everyone's blood pressure.

2. *The Accountability Approach.* Think back to when you were in school. Do you remember when your teacher

would call out "Time for a pop quiz"? Whether or not you'd done your reading the night before directly affected how much you sweated it during that quiz. This is the accountability approach briefly. It's simply a checkup on you to verify that you've done the things you should be doing.

3. *The Thinking Approach* is close to Socrates' method when he engaged others in his philosophical questioning exercises. People's knowledge and critical thinking were tested with profound questions. For example, a law school professor might ask, "Ms. Greene, were the plaintiff's first amendments rights violated when she

was prevented from joining other cheerleaders on the football field until after the national anthem had been concluded due to her refusal to stand during the anthem?" The professor will also ask the students to extrapolate beyond their readings to apply theories and principles in advanced ways. For example, "Ms. Greene, does your response change in any way if I tell you that the plaintiff was attending a private university instead of a public state university?"

Question Examples for a Socratic Dialogue

In *The Thinker's Guide to the Art of Socratic Questioning,* published in 2006 by Richard Paul and Linda Elder, the authors summarized 8 (later extended to 9) categories where one can ask Socratic questions effectively. [xxvii] The following list is aimed to help you expand your vocabulary on how do Socratic questions sound like:

"1. **Questions of Clarification.**

- What is your main point … ?

- What do you mean by …?

- Could you give me an example?

- Could you explain that further?

2. Questions That Probe Purpose.

- What was your purpose when you said …?

- What is the purpose of the main character in this story?

- Was this purpose justifiable?

- What is the purpose of addressing this question at this time?

3. Questions That Probe Assumptions

- What are you assuming?

- What could we assume instead?

- You seem to be assuming … . Do I understand you correctly?

- Is it always the case? Why do you think the assumption holds here?

4. Questions That Probe Information, Reasons, Evidence, and Causes.

- What would be an example?

- How do you know?

- Why do you think that is true?

- Is this good evidence for believing that?

5. Questions about Viewpoints or Perspectives.

  • You seem to be approaching this issue from … perspective. Why have you chosen this perspective rather than that perspective?

  • How would other groups or types of people respond? Why? What would influence them?

  • How could you answer the objection that … would make?

  • Can/did anyone see this another way?

6. Questions That Probe Implications and Consequences.

  • What are you implying by that?

  • When you say … , are you implying?

- What effect would that have?

- What is an alternative?

7. Questions about the Question

- How can we find out?

- Is this the same issue as … ?

- How could someone settle this question?

- What does this question assume?

8. Questions That Probe Concepts

- What is the main idea we are dealing with?

- Why/how this idea is important?

- Do these two ideas conflict? If so, how?

• What was the main idea guiding the character's thinking in this story?

9. Questions That Probe Inferences and Interpretations.

• Which conclusions are we coming to about…?

• On what information are we basing this conclusion?

• Is there a more logical inference we might make in this situation?

• How are you interpreting her behavior? Is there another possible interpretation?"[xxviii]

This is an abundant list of questions. Warren Berger, an American journalist, and the author of

The Book of Beautiful Questions pinned down five essential questions one can ask to improve their critical thinking and understanding.

How can I see this from a new perspective?

What am I assuming?

What conclusion am I rushing?

What am I not seeing?

What is the most important part here?[xxix]

These questions can serve as a quickfire self-checking tool you can use before engaging in a Socratic dialogue. By examining your thought process, you decrease the chances of hidden biases and assumptions. Your thinking becomes clearer, and your argument more valid.

Chapter 2: On Ethics and Virtue.

Ethics was at the heart of Socrates' agenda. He was invested in defining and distinguishing right from wrong. This, again, was a tricky undertaking as what's right for one person may not be right for another. Socrates was on the lookout for an objective good that must be so under any circumstance. It's like the Kantian categorical imperative, which is "an unconditional moral obligation which is binding in all circumstances and is not dependent on a person's inclination or purpose."[xxx]

Finding such objective truths is challenging because virtually everything good for someone can be detrimental for someone else. While a coal mine is horrible for the environment and the local community, it is good for the owners of the mine and all those people the coal will serve. Giving your seat up for the elderly is good for that person, but it may be detrimental to you if the bus suddenly breaks and you fall. These are examples of good or bad phenomena, not the definition of an overarching concept, as Socrates would wish. But how can we define what good precedes other goods? How can we tell for certain what's objectively good?

These questions take us to the more abstract territory of virtues. In the previous chapter, we discussed that Aristotle, a student of Plato, gleaned much information about Socrates due to Plato's relationship with Socrates. We can reason it to be a fairly accurate assessment of Socrates' actions, abilities, and analysis of big life questions, i.e., what is virtue? What is justice? Unlike other philosophers, Socrates emphatically claimed that he never taught, and his personal style of philosophizing was through conversation.[xxxi]

Because Socrates' work as a philosopher was preserved in this unique way, there are no published works by Socrates we can look at and analyze to learn more about his pondering on virtues. However, one of Plato's contemporary philosophers and a follower of Socrates, Xenophon, compiled many of Socrates' conversations and exchanges in his book *Memorabilia*.

In Xenophon's book, we can see a pattern of topics Socrates would discuss repeatedly.

These topics included searching for the truth, the definition of justice, knowledge, virtue, and finding the objective good. Socrates focused on the consistency of his performance as he has continued to discuss the same topics and continued saying the same things about them, not wavering in his stance a single time.

Socrates' agenda included encouraging individuals to care for their soul and to make it as pure as possible. This is an interesting topic considering Socrates' own viewpoint of atheism and his subsequent charges for impiety.

In Socrates' beliefs, depraved actions are committed due to a lack of knowledge; it is better to be the victim of injustice rather than commit an injustice. Many of Socrates' conversations discuss how a person "should" or "ought" to live. This is one of the most commonly repeating themes in Socrates' list of topics. The ethics of life appears in his conversations more than in any other area of philosophy.

Even today, spending time in deep thought considering how one "ought" to live is not a common pastime. Most people live their lives by the standards they grew up with and exist as part of their cultural or societal norms. In Socrates' opinion, individuals need to question and challenge these norms rather than follow them blindly. Taking the time to scrutinize how one lives and deeply think about the answer can have a profound effect. This practice can be done day by day, allowing individuals to make positive choices as their lives change based on the new knowledge.

Practicing this analysis requires self-knowledge. The individual has to look inward and analyze their nature and values. Socrates himself said, "The unexamined life is not worth living."[xxxii] Taking stock of who you are is one of the best decisions you can make. By engaging in this practice, you will learn, at a minimum, how you are living your life and how does it compare to the life you would like to live. Once you have that information, you can consciously decide how to best care for yourself going forward.

Socrates famously said, "Our true self is our soul."[xxxiii] Because Socrates lived before the Christian Era, it's difficult to know what he means by soul, but there is a clear understanding the term lacks the significance tied to the religious aspect used. According to Socrates, "It is the state of our soul or inner being, which determines our quality of life."[xxxiv] However, in contradiction to this, most people believe they can identify what type of things are heavenly and evil.[xxxv] Generally, wealth, social acceptance, power, and status are universally good and signs of success. Poverty, social rejection, pain, and death are considered outward signs of evil. Over time this will be proven to be untrue. However, having a false idea of what makes a person happy can lead to indiscriminately chasing that thing to be "happy" or achieve inner peace. But once that goal has been reached, the person realizes attaining an item or status won't change how they feel. Self-knowledge brings happiness and peace of mind.

To Socrates, the greatest good possible was virtue, demonstrated when a person shows moral excellence. A virtuous person actively engages in virtuous behavior while maintaining positive moral character. The cardinal virtues include wisdom, justice, courage, and temperance.[xxxvi] A good demonstration of Socratic questioning would be if you would question, "is courage one of the highest virtues?" And then pursue an argument with someone until both of you can agree on a definition.

Virtue was a commonly discussed topic for Socrates. He believed that when a person correctly defined virtue, they would naturally have to see its true value as the greatest good, which would lead them to happiness as they performed the "good" task. This happiness would then automatically lead the person to behave in a virtuous manner.

Essentially, Socrates' thoughts can be expressed like this: *Knowledge => Virtue => Happiness.*

One of the key problems with Socrates' theory is that if happiness is so easy to attain, why do many people choose not to become virtuous and prefer to engage in evil acts? The philosopher's answer is "because a lot of people are ignorant." To Socrates, individuals engaging in evil acts don't realize what they're doing is evil. If they did, they wouldn't engage in those behaviors. Since these evil acts are committed out of ignorance, they are done involuntarily, giving the individual no free will to decide either way.

In Plato's writing we see Socrates stating that individuals who commit evil acts fail to realize that behaving in a virtuous manner is the greatest possible good and that being virtuous will bring them happiness. Instead, Socrates believes people fall into the trap of committing evil acts because they falsely believe privileges like wealth, power, and pleasure are the best goods that exist. The evil acts are committed to gain those privileges. In Socrates' worldview, the person who engages in evil acts doesn't realize he's besmirching his soul and putting himself on a path to perpetual misery. The cluelessness of not recognizing what will make one happy starts a cycle of bad behavior that repeats itself as the person thinks they know what will make them happy but never experiences that fulfillment.

Interestingly, this is a concept many criminals have brought into the modern era as they've tried to justify their crimes to themselves and others. It has also been a way to mitigate guilt so the perpetrator can feel better about their involvement in the crime. Or simply tell themselves whatever they needed to hear to make having committed the criminal act something they can live with.[xxxvii] The most common themes used to justify a criminal's illegal actions include:

Denial of responsibility" is when an offender proposes that they were forced by the circumstances they were in to commit a crime; "denial of injury" means insisting that the crime was harmless; "denial of the victim" involves the belief that the person on the receiving end was asking for it; and "condemnation of the condemners" is when the criminal claims those criticizing or dishing out punishment are doing so out of spite or to shift the blame from themselves. The final method, "appealing to higher loyalties," involves the perpetrator believing that the law needs to be broken for the good of a smaller section of society—for example, a gang or a group of friends.[xxxviii]

Besides justifying crimes, we've also learned through the study of the brain that the criminal mind isn't all that different from the non-criminal mind. Think back to any news broadcast you may have seen recently about serial killers. Joseph James DeAngelo, the Golden State Killer, was recently identified through a controversial familial DNA match after one of his relatives voluntarily submitted DNA to a commercial genomics company. From the outside looking in, Joseph DeAngelo seemed normal. He was married in 1973 and had three daughters. However, during that time, DeAngelo also committed thirteen murders and over fifty rapes, earning him the name, the Golden State Killer.[xxxix]

When people think about the monster who committed the horrible and disturbing crimes, there is a strong idea this person must set themselves apart somehow, but more often than not, what we see is the ability to hide in plain sight. This was not a skill unique to Joseph DeAngelo. Other serial killers had this same ability to charm their way out of difficult situations. Ted Bundy worked at a crisis hotline for people contemplating suicide with the now-famous true crime author Anne Rule.[xl] Doctor Harold Shipman had a clinical practice comprised mostly of elderly women, where he injected them with large doses of painkillers to murder them so he could gain access to their money.[xli] These people, and many more, committed evil acts yet seemed normal. Your average everyday citizen. Sometimes, the individuals posed as someone injured or needing assistance to gain their victim's trust and sympathy. Thanks to them, we learned that appearances couldn't be taken for granted as a true marker of identity and personality.

Back to Socrates and virtues. To properly question and converse on virtues, one must know their own heart and soul. How could we claim we know who we are if we don't question our beliefs? How does our right, good, and virtuous compare to someone else's? What yardstick do we use to measure our truths?

Practice the examined life.

It's important that you take Socrates' advice and discover who you are on the inside. Examine your inner world and your values. This will be the start of a lifelong journey of self-discovery. Just don't anticipate having life all figured out in one go. Trying to answer life's big questions takes a lot of time and disciplined self-discovery.

Getting to know yourself is the ongoing process of understanding who you—the human —really are on a much deeper level than the surface. The goal is to get at what motivates you and how you see and interpret things internally. Depending on what this may also mean, taking the plunge and embracing your insecurities, self-doubt, and anything else that prevents you from putting your life under a microscope for a full and thorough examination.[xlii]

This is not an easy task. It takes dedication and commitment, but the rewards gleaned from self-examination and knowing your values and what you want to achieve in life are worth the hard work. Once you know what is truly important to you, you'll be able to live by those values and beliefs and ensure others respect them. Knowing yourself this intimately allows you to prioritize things based on who you are. You'll have a different level of respect for your body and treat it with the kindness it deserves.[xliii]

There are numerous benefits to knowing yourself. You'll know where you excel in life and where you could use some additional work to reach your goals. Knowing who you are means you'll know all about your personality quirks and that you won't let them stop you from discovering your life's purpose.[xliv]

The idea that you've grown up and subsequently aged with yourself and therefore must know yourself on the most fundamental levels is a false narrative. Such a complicated endeavor as learning about your core self requires intentionality. Ask yourself:

Why do I exist?

What is my purpose in life?

What are my values and how do they shape my life?

These questions take time to think about and work through. It's crucial that you don't simply mimic cultural and societal norms passed down by your parents and environment. You get to decide what is important to you and create your own set of values to live by.

So, getting to know yourself… how do you do that exactly? That's a great question! In Socrates' practice there are five categories you need to know about yourself. You will gain insight how you fit in these categories based on the questions designed to help you reach the goal of looking inward and learning more about who you are.[xlv]

1. Get to know your personality

To your best knowledge, how do other people perceive you?

How confident are you in your ability to make decisions for yourself?

What brings you joy?

What gifts do you bring?

Why does the world need the gifts you bring?

Who needs the gifts you bring?

What verb best describes you?

When do you feel the most like yourself?

What makes you feel great about yourself?

What kinds of conversations do you have with your closest friends?

2. Get to know your core values

What is your highest core value?

What is your biggest self-limiting belief?

Who is the most important person in your life?

What is something that is true for you no matter what?

What is your moral compass in making difficult decisions?

What gives your life meaning?

What's missing from your life? From the world?

What do other people always thank you for?

What are you willing to struggle for?

3. Get to know your body

How comfortable are you with your own mortality?

What's memorable about you?

What makes you lose track of time?

4. Get to know your dreams

What kind of legacy do you want to leave behind?

What is one failure you have turned into your greatest lesson?

How is life calling you?

If money wasn't an issue, what would you do with your time?

What kind of person do you want to be in five years?

What did you imagine you'd be doing right now when you were fifteen years old?

Who inspires you most? What qualities do they possess that inspire you?

5. Get to know your likes and dislikes

How would you like others to perceive you?

How do you want to make others feel?

If you had to teach something, what would you teach?

What makes you smile?

What are you drawn to?[xlvi]

Take your time to answer these questions. If you are inclined to skip one, pay attention to that urge. Why do you feel you want to jump over that question? This simple awareness about your mind's inner workings will provide you with good insight into who you are.

Know-What, Know-How, and Know-Why.

The main purpose of Socratic questioning is to discover *the truth* by asking strategic and impactful questions. This sometimes can be a challenging endeavor. Why does the Earth orbit the sun? Because the sun's gravity keeps the Earth in its orbit.

That's a scientifically factual response. However, addressing a question such as "Why do we exist?" is more difficult. There is no factual response to it. However, three types of knowledge can facilitate answering even the more challenging questions. These three "knowledges" are: "know what, know how, and know why."[xlvii]

In the "know what" concept of knowledge, we can pinpoint things we know because we have empirical evidence. "Know what" follows the principle of learning-by-using. The questions we ask are closed-ended to quickly verify the factual response. "I know that in Austria, deciduous trees shed their leaves in the autumn and bloom in spring." Or, "I know that my readers prefer books over blog posts." The answers respond to questions such as, "What do deciduous trees do in Austria?" or "Do your readers prefer books over blogposts?" These questions have one correct answer based on previous studies and analyses.

"Know how" is a learning-by-doing based on skill development. People aren't born with the ability to acquire a skill instantly. It takes time and practice to learn any new craft. Think about learning to play a musical instrument. You have to learn to read sheet music, place your fingers on the instruments, and play in proper pitch and time with the rest of the band. The point is, "know how" requires developing a skill via a specific process. For example, you could ask, "how do you know what deciduous trees do in Austria?" The answer might be, "I observed that deciduous trees shed their leaves in the autumn and reborn in spring for more than fifty years. And so did many people before me. Each year, the same cycle repeats itself. It's a conclusion based on the observation of pattern repetition." Another example would be, "how do you know your readers prefer books over blogposts?" The answer would sound like, "I poll my readership at the end of each year about their reading preference. Furthermore, I compare the data in my Google Analytics tracking blogpost visits to my book sales data. More people purchase my books than visit my website." As you can see, both answers describe a type of skill – observation over time and data analysis. Asking a "know how" question expanded our knowledge on how people know what they claim they know.

The final concept of knowledge is "know why," or learning-by-studying. Beyond curiosity-driven questioning, it "involves controlled experimentation and simulation to understand the principles and theories underlying" the study subject. The question, "Why do deciduous trees behave the way they do in Austria?" could take one's knowledge a step further. "Austria has a continental climate with warm summers and cold winters. Deciduous trees shed leaves to prepare for the harsh winter temperatures. They also grow in places with wet and dry climates. In those areas, they shed their leaves in the dry season. Deciduous trees' behavior revolves around the sun. Once trees sense a dropping in daylight, they start to reduce how much chlorophyll (the green pigment responsible for absorbing light) they produce. With the coming of cold, trees shed leaves to conserve their resources."[xlviii]

Asking "Why do you think readers prefer books over blogposts?" helps the author to become more curious about their readers' behavior. Answering this question can help the author improve his performance. Once we ask why, we have opened ourselves up to the primary goal of Socratic questioning. But this is only step one. We must first look for patterns – similar events and results over an extended time or geographic location to claim this hypothesis is the truth. Additionally, we can conduct simulations that bring about the same results, strengthening the argument. The first written observations of deciduous trees would hardly have been considered facts. The consistent and repeating pattern observation of tree behavior in places with a similar climate brought more clarity and certainty about the correct explanation. Know-why is an immersive type of learning.

Chapter 3: Persuade Others With Socratic Questioning

The Truth vs. Persuasion

When we use the Socratic method as a persuasion tool, we distance ourselves from its original meaning. Socrates didn't want to persuade others to see things as he did. He wanted to encourage a learning discussion. When we ask persuasive questions, we intend to change the other person's mind.

Questioning to persuade others is done in the same fashion as regular Socratic questioning with a caveat. These questions are less open-ended and usually are suggestive of an answer. "What do you think about bicycles?" and "Do you like bicycles?" sound like the same question at first read. But if you look deeper, the first question doesn't influence what you think about bicycles. The second question injects the word "like" into the picture. Now, you can still say, "no, I don't like bicycles." But if you asked 1,000 people, more would say "yes" than if you asked them, "what do you think about bicycles?"

Persuasion using the Socratic method can be more intense – like the bootcamp approach we talked about in the first chapter – or less intense – like the thinking approach. Let's see an example of an intense persuasive argument between Rachel and Rick:

Rachel: The dog cannot sleep in the bed.

Rick: Can you hear the dog crying when he doesn't sleep in the bed? It keeps me up at night. Don't you want me to get a good night's rest?

Rachel: He gets dog hair on the bed, and I don't like that.

Rick: If I brush the dog more often and change the bed sheets more frequently, would that make having the dog in the bed more tolerable for you?

Rachel: I suppose we can try it. But you must brush him and change the sheets. If you don't, he can't stay in bed.

In the above example, Rick's goal is to convince Rachel to allow their dog to sleep in their bed. Rick is giving her a guilt trip at first by saying that the dog cries and he can't sleep well. Then he follows that up by agreeing to do some extra work so there won't be so much dog hair in the bed.

Now let's see a milder case of a persuasive Socratic conversation on the topic of breastfeeding in public. In the United States, breastfeeding in public is legal in all 50 states. However, periodically, news stories reference nursing mothers being asked to leave public areas (shopping malls, restaurants, pools, playgrounds) for being indecent. In the scenario below, Jane, a new mother, is nursing her newborn child in a restaurant while joining her friends Amy and Beth for lunch.

Amy: I don't know how you can do that in public. I would be too embarrassed and think everyone was looking at me.

Jane: I'm feeding my son. He's two months old, and it's natural. Isn't this what breasts are for? If other people are eating in this restaurant, why is it inappropriate for my child to eat here too?

Beth: I never thought of it from that viewpoint. I agree that telling women to nurse in a bathroom is harsh, but how do you explain what's happening to other children in the restaurant? This is a family establishment.

Jane: But what exactly is visible to the public? You really can't see anything, can you? I try hard to be discreet. If it bothers someone, can't they simply look away? How is my child eating in public any different than anyone else eating in public? It makes no logical sense. Do those same parents complain to the publishers about magazine covers they see with cleavage on them? Don't children see those too?

Amy: Aren't you worried someone might call the police?

Beth: That's true. What are you going to do if you get arrested for indecent exposure? You could have a criminal record.

Jane: Breastfeeding in public is exempt from those laws and is legal in all 50 states. I understand this is a choice and not everyone is comfortable with it, but I support and believe in it.

Beth: Can't you just use a breast pump? Wouldn't that be simpler?

Jane: Not really. Those can take a lot of time, are expensive, and have to be cleaned.

Amy: Well, this conversation has been enlightening. What are we all going to eat?

Here, we see Jane responding to Amy's and Beth's questions with statements and questions designed to make the women think about her viewpoint as a nursing mother. In turn, Amy and Beth ask Jane questions that ask her to consider the larger public view. In this conversation, Jane isn't aiming to get Amy and Beth to agree breastfeeding in public is the right decision for them, nor are Amy and Beth telling Jane she should not breastfeed in public. Instead, we see Jane expressing her reasons in a persuasive style due to her knowledge on this topic. She has *justified* reasons for her opinions she can articulate to others. Yet Jane is not on a proverbial soapbox, preaching that her beliefs are the only acceptable ones.

Key Steps to Effectively and Morally Improve Your Persuasion Skills[xlix]

Step 1. Mimic Socrates

There's a saying that proposes imitation is the highest form of flattery. Generally, statements and facts will garner arguments when attempting to persuade others. Even if you do thorough research and are prepared, someone will challenge the validity of what you're saying. Instead of throwing facts at people, ask questions that drift their focus on your viewpoint, just like Socrates did.

For example, if you present to a group of engineers with data and reports that the number one hazard on the roadways in your town over the next five years will be unsafe bridges, be prepared for those engineers to suggest that everything from drunk drivers to potholes are far more unsafe. On the other hand, if you ask questions like, "When was the last time the bridges in this area were properly serviced and inspected?" "What is the maximum weight each bridge can handle at any given time, and how much weight is crossing these bridges during the times of heaviest traffic?" and "What is the average cost to bring each bridge up to modern standard versus the potential loss of life if the bridges collapse?" the engineers in the room will be focusing on attempting to respond to those questions.

Step 2: Determine What Facts You Already Assume

When thinking about what questions you want to ask, acknowledge what facts you already assume are true. In the first example regarding the bridges, the questions were framed, so it already assumed that the bridges were unsafe and needed to be updated. Therefore, no questions were asking about the basic premise. You want to ask questions that support your position in a persuasive argument.

Step 3: Turn Assumptions into Questions

Make sure that when you turn your assumptions into questions, you will get the answer you want. Let's say you work in a school that provides the same breakfast and lunch to all its students, aged from 4 years old to 14 years old. Some of the older children have complained the portions are too small, and they are often hungry during the day. At the next staff meeting, you bring these questions to be answered:

- Are the daily caloric needs of a 4-year-old and a 14-year-old the same?

- Do we expect children to get the most from a classroom learning environment when they are hungry?

- Do we know that most students in our school get most of their calories here due to the low socioeconomic status of the school?

These questions demonstrate the need for older children to receive a larger portioned meal for breakfast and lunch. Board members already know the answers to these questions. You simply strategically phrase the assumptions in a manner to have others in the staff meeting think about why this will be necessary for older children. If you simply exclaimed with your sword out, "let's give bigger meals for older children," you may have encountered resistance.

Step 4: Did You Miss an Assumption?

When you go through the Socratic questioning process to be persuasive, you have to hit all the right chords. It's possible to miss an assumption on either the emotional or logical level.

Let's say you are requesting your employer to provide a free flu shot clinic at your office so employees can quickly and efficiently receive the flu vaccine. You may ask as one of your assumptions, "Don't you care about the health of the employees who work for you?" Your employer may respond by informing you that he's far more interested in productivity. So now, you must frame your questions around how the flu shot can reduce or prevent time away from the office.

Step 5: What if You're Just Wrong?

You might have made a mistake and what you thought was an issue isn't. There's no shame in realizing this and moving on to other areas of your job that need your attention. It's the mature approach. However, if you are still passionate about whatever you were advocating, you must find another way for others to agree with your approach.

Let's look back at the issue regarding portion sizes for older children. Before implementing what was an overall good idea (increasing portion sizes), the families of the older students were polled and surveyed about this matter. The responses found that students who were still hungry brought additional snacks at school to help curb their appetite, so larger portions would be wasteful. However, about 25% of respondents indicated that additional portions would be useful.

Because of the survey, you may come up with a happy medium solution. It would be better to implement a policy whereby students with unused prepackaged items and whole fruit, juice, and milk left over from their breakfast and lunch trays could donate those back to the school. These items would then be available for any child who wanted an additional item to help complete their meal. This program helped reduce waste and cost no additional money.

When to Use Persuasive Socratic Questioning

Highly effective salespeople use Socratic questioning techniques to persuade others to buy whatever product they sell. Let's look at the classic example of a car salesman. They usually ask a potential customer questions such as:

- Are you looking for a new car for your family?
- What price range do you want to stay in?
- Are you planning to trade in the car you drove into the lot today?
- Where do you want your monthly payments to be?

- What kinds of features are important to you?
- Does the car have to be an SUV or sport wagon?
- Will you be financing the car you purchase?

As you can see, some questions assume that the customer will be purchasing a car and that it will be from that specific dealer. The questions about financing, trade-in, and monthly payments allow the dealer to estimate how much the buyer will be spending on a particular car (i.e. the salesman isn't showing BMWs to someone who can afford a Kia). The customer's answers to these questions allow the salesman to showcase the best options in stock that meet these qualifications and persuade the buyer to make a final purchase.

Another question commonly asked in sales is "Don't you deserve it?" or "Don't you want your family to have the best?" This is a very persuasive question, and it's a trap that many people will fall into because, with their family, they do want the best. They want their children to be protected by dual-side airbags or to have that entertainment system in the back so they can watch movies on road trips. Remember that while you may use these tricks, stay aware of them potentially being used on you.

Is it fair?

One classic characteristic of a Socratic question is the lack of a single correct answer. The methodology challenges how you think about things, especially challenging issues, and teaches you to ask questions and think critically. One of the easiest and most practical ways to get started using the Socratic method is to simply ask an open-ended question, ask follow-up questions based on what you learn, and then utilize what you've learned.

I will use the Socratic method to challenge whether the more restrictive dress codes for young women in a K–12 public school setting are appropriate compared to their male counterparts. This topic became controversial in the past decade. Dress codes have forbidden young women from showing their shoulders, collarbones, or knees, wearing shorts or skirts at some designated improper level, and the list goes on. The reason many schools have communicated these stifling and Victorian-era dress codes is often attributed to the school's male population. The school demands their female students to hide any aspect of their womanhood a man might find pleasing, as that man cannot control his urges, and he will be distracted by the female in her less-than-acceptable attire.

The reasoning and justifications for these stringent policies that objectify women are insulting to young women and men. When employing Socratic questioning concerning dress codes such as this, questions to ask would include:

- Is the administration suggesting that young men cannot control themselves around young women?
- Are women humans who may dress reasonably and appropriately for the weather?

(e.g. men can wear tank tops to school, but women may not) Or are women objects that exist to be pleasing to the eye or sexual gratification?

- Why is all the responsibility for "distracting men" placed on women versus teaching men that staring at women is inappropriate or teaching them concentration techniques?

- Does the administration realize that, in the end, under any amount of material, young men and women are still experiencing puberty, and it is likely that the hormones of their age that is driving their distraction far more than their clothing?

- How does the school rectify allowing cheerleaders or other sports participants to wear uniforms during school spirit days when those uniforms violate dress code?

These are just a few questions asked in real dress code cases recently. These issues have included disparaging both male and female students over what they wear. Out of frustration, both students and their parents voiced that the dress codes had gotten ridiculous. Most students and their parents felt that the schools were imposing draconian policies, particularly on female students, while male students were treated as if they lacked the mental capacity to accept personal responsibility for their behavior—which the male students were not a fan of either. By asking these questions at school board meetings and on news broadcasts, teens and their parents hoped to raise these issues for an honest discussion so reasonable policies could be implemented.

Chapter 4: Socratic Questioning and Cognitive Behavioral Therapy.

I am not a therapist, and I am not representing myself as one either. This chapter means to discuss the many uses of the Socratic method for therapists or those who seek the services of a therapist. Counseling and therapy can be priceless for helping you navigate a difficult period in your life.

It takes time for the patient-doctor relationship to develop enough trust to divulge the real reason they seek therapy. It's not uncommon for a patient to state they are seeking therapy for one reason, but later reveal they are in therapy for a related but deeper issue. An example of this might ask to discuss their lack of organization skills and later may reveal that they are, in actuality, a hoarder whose home is overrun by junk and garbage. Socratic questioning used in therapy sessions can help both the therapist and patient identify the true purpose of therapy sooner rather than later.

Admitting deeply personal things about yourself is difficult. However, a good therapist can use cognitive restructuring to help you change your thoughts and later your actions related to a problematic life area. According to Therapist Aid, "Cognitive restructuring refers to the process of challenging and changing irrational thoughts. Socratic questioning is one technique to encourage this process. Therapists use Socratic questioning verbally by asking probing questions about their clients' irrational thoughts. As clients improve their awareness of irrational thoughts, they can begin to consciously question their thoughts."[1]

By using Socratic questioning in therapy sessions, the therapist's goal is to assist the patient in determining which thoughts are irrational and lead the patient down a path of problem behaviors. The therapist then works with the patient to help them identify these thoughts independently, so the individual can unlearn old behaviors and learn new ones.

How to Use the Socratic Method Effectively in Therapy Sessions

Collaborative Empiricism

When someone goes to therapy for any reason, who ensures that they reach their goals? You may think it is the therapist being paid for their services. Perhaps you think the patient has to ultimately put in the work to experience meaningful life changes. In cognitive behavioral therapy, the concept of the collaborative theory states that both the patient and the therapist must work together to achieve therapy goals. On the one hand, the therapist needs to ask insightful, well-thought-out, and sensitive questions to determine why the patient engages in undesirable thoughts or behaviors. On the other hand, the patient will need to test the therapist's hypothesis. Then it is up to the patient to practice what they learn in therapy and step on the path of change. The therapist needs to respect the patient's autonomy during this process, as it will continue to foster a trusting relationship between them.[li]

Guided Discovery

Guided discovery is when the therapist assists the patient with discovering their collection of beliefs and opinions. In cognitive therapy, the therapist focuses on information the patient discloses during their therapy sessions. In guided discovery, the therapist uses Socratic questioning to bring the patient's thoughts into hyper focus rather than offering insight to solving a particular problem. The Socratic method is a significant part of guided discovery because it allows the therapist to engage patients to learn useful information and then process that information to benefit the patient's therapy. The therapist must engage with the patient in a conversational manner. This way, the therapist can help the patient pinpoint beliefs and opinions based on incorrect information and have the patient consider other options that may improve their circumstances. Soon we will walk through two examples that illustrate this interaction between patient and therapist. [lii]

Making the Most Out of Socratic Questioning

Besides maintaining a collaborative stance when working with patients, it's crucial to create a safe, judgment-free environment for them. One way the therapist can implement this is to be curious. Being inquisitive and asking questions over assuming that they already know a patient's beliefs and opinions are will lead to genuine discovery and connection. Without curiosity, a therapist may miss out on the real backstory of a client's thought process contributing to their dysfunctional behavior.

Example of Socratic Questioning in a Therapy Session: Family Issue

Therapist: How are you, Eve? So, today we're talking through a situation where you feel as if your mother-in-law ignored you. You told her something, and she didn't respond. And you think it is because she doesn't like you, right? So, I thought we'd maybe do a little bit of dialogue back and forth. I could ask you questions about what happened and how you feel about the situation. This is called Socratic questioning. Is that okay with you if we dive into this?

Eve: That's fine.

Therapist: Okay. Do you think your mother-in-law doesn't like you?

Eve: Yeah.

Therapist: Why do you think she doesn't like you? What else might she be thinking?

Eve: Well, my husband and I just got married, and we've been living with my in-laws for about a month. He is between jobs... A few days ago, I walked into the house and said hello and asked her if she needed anything, but she ignored me. It was like I wasn't even there. So, you know, I'm thinking, "Yeah, she doesn't like me, she's kind of a jerk."

Therapist: Okay. So you feel your mother-in-law ignores you on purpose. And that she's kind of a jerk.

Eve: Yes. Exactly.

Therapist: Right. Which one feels stronger, more accurate? Should we think about it right now?

Eve: She ignores me because she doesn't like me.

Therapist: "She doesn't like me." You're focused on that today. Are you assuming how your mother-in-law feels about you based on that one interaction?

Eve: I guess... Because if she liked me, she would acknowledge me.

Therapist: Okay.

Eve: But yes. I built my assumption based on that one interaction.

Therapist: Right. Do you think that acknowledging you means someone likes you and not acknowledging you means they don't?

Eve: When you phrase it like that, it sounds rather black or white.

Therapist: Indeed. Do you think your mother-in-law could have had any other reason for not acknowledging you?

Eve: It's possible she didn't hear me. She was reading a book when I came into the room. I was loud, so she should have heard me, but she could have been focused on her reading.

Therapist: That's a viable alternative assumption.

Eve: I guess I'm assuming she heard me because I was standing close to her.

Therapist: There are a couple of things that stand out here. Based on your assumptions, you're certain that your mother-in-law heard you asking a question and ignored you willfully because she doesn't like you. Do you have any evidence this is true?

Eve: The evidence would be the lack of acknowledgement. I don't know. Sometimes, she can be a little cold toward me. So yes, I think it's because she doesn't like me.

Therapist: Why did you conclude that? What made you think that was the best option?

Eve: I could have looked at it differently. Like I said, she might have just been absorbed in her book. She's an avid reader. Or maybe she was stressed out and didn't realize I was there. She could have been tired from work too.

Therapist: Those are all possible reasons she may not have responded to you. When we have all these viable reasons your mother-in-law didn't acknowledge you, why did you settle on because she didn't like you?

Eve: I didn't think of all the other reasons.

Therapist: But you are now? What is it that you're thinking?

Eve: That perhaps I judged too quickly, and I should have been more open-minded.

Therapist: Now go back to your first inclination, "She doesn't like me." When you think that and hang on to that as the reason your mother-in-law didn't acknowledge you, how does it make you feel?

Eve: I feel depressed and lonely. Like I can't talk to my mother-in-law any longer.

Therapist: What about when we consider the other possibilities for why you weren't acknowledged? How do those possibilities make you feel?

Eve: If one of them were the real reason my mother-in-law ignored me, I'd know it wasn't about me, and I'd feel relieved. I would feel happy, I suppose, because everything I was worried about would be gone.

Therapist: Do you think having this conversation has helped you consider alternative reasons your mother-in-law might not have responded to you?

Eve: Absolutely, it's made me look at what happened and think about things differently.

Therapist: And now that you're considering that you weren't willfully ignored, how does that make you feel on an emotional level?

Eve: Surprised. It makes me wonder why I didn't think of alternative options before. I just latched onto the idea that my mother-in-law hated me now that I had married her son. In my family, the persona of the hateful mother-in-law was a running joke. My maternal grandmother disliked my dad. She considered him unworthy of my mom. I thought all mother-in-laws would feel that way.

Therapist: Now that's a very interesting observation there…

Example of Socratic Questioning in a Therapy Session: Dating and Resiliency

Let's examine another example where the therapist asks Socratic questioning-infused cognitive behavioral therapy questions.

Therapist: How are things going on the dating front?

Tom: Not particularly well. I've gone on a lot of first dates. I think they go well, but when I ask the women out for a second date, they don't answer my calls or return my messages or texts. I've pretty much decided to stop dating.

Therapist: That is a significant decision.
              Let's talk about it. When did
              you make this decision?

Tom: Last Tuesday. I tried to call the
              woman I took out on a date on
              Friday night to let her know I'd
              had a good time and to see if
              she wanted to go out again, and
              she said she just wasn't
              interested.

Therapist: So, when your most recent date
              stated she wasn't interested in
              continuing to see you, is that
              when you gave up hope?

Tom: Yeah. I remember thinking I
              could take no more rejection.
              I've had many dates over the
              past year since Allison and I

broke up, and they never go anywhere. It makes me feel like a social pariah.

Therapist: I can imagine that's been difficult for you, especially reentering the dating scene after a long-term relationship. Can you think of anything positive coming out of dating for you?

Tom: I can't think of anything. It's been almost a year since I started dating again, and I don't think I've made any second dates, let alone anything even resembling a solid relationship.

Therapist: How many dates do you estimate you've been on since you started dating again?

Tom: I don't know. An average of once a week for the last year, so 52… I guess.

Therapist: I can see that you've taken dating seriously and put in much effort. But the important question here is whether it's worth it to continue dating. How many dates do you think the average person has to find the person they want to be in a relationship with?

Tom: I'd probably imagine it could be 25 or 30, but I suppose it could take more.

Therapist: So, considering that information, does 52 dates seem wholly unreasonable? Do you know anyone who dated more people than 25 or 30 or even 52?

Tom: Well, I have a buddy who was a bit of a playboy. I'd assumed he was a confirmed bachelor as he was dating a different woman every time I saw him, but lo and behold he met the love of his life one day and settled down with her quickly after they met. He'd been dating around for years before he met her.

Therapist: Really? That sounds like an important piece of information. What if your friend had come to you after a year of dating and said he wasn't going to date any longer because he hadn't met "the one" yet?

Tom: I probably would have told him he was silly and that it takes time to meet the right person. It's kind of like a needle in a haystack, and not to give up.

Therapist: I think that sounds like reasonable advice. I know it's hard to remember that, especially after several disappointments. Do you think your advice also applies to your situation?

Tom: I suppose it does.

Therapist: So, what can you do to help you remember this, so you don't get discouraged about dating?

Tom: I suppose I could write a note to myself and keep it on my cellphone so it will be easy to pull up. If things don't work out after future dates, the note can remind me that searching for someone to share your life with is like searching for a needle in a haystack and not being discouraged if this person didn't work out because there are plenty of fish in the sea.

Therapist: That's an excellent idea. So now let's talk about some reasons you may not be getting acceptance when you ask women out on second dates.

Tom: Good deal.

The Therapist Aid provides questions that anyone applying the Socratic method can clarify their thinking. Besides answering the questions below, elaborate on your answer and indicate why or why not. [liii]

In the example below, we will pick up where the prior example left off in Tom's therapy session and then address the questions as if Tom was responding.

<u>Thought to Be Questioned</u>: I cannot successfully carry any first dates into a second date.

<u>*What is the evidence for this thought? Against it?*</u>

I have been on approximately 52 dates in the past year, and none have led to a second date despite my attempts to contact my dates within a reasonable time, saying I had a good time—and seemingly, they also enjoyed the date.

Am I basing this thought on facts or feelings?

Probably both. It is factual that none of my first dates have led to second dates, but there is an emotional component of rejection involved after each rejection. It's possible that after a certain amount of rejection, my bitterness and resentment infiltrated my later dates, and I did not realize this.

Could I be misinterpreting the evidence? Am I making any assumptions?

I don't think so. Sure, were we talking about a smaller group of women, that's a definite possibility. However, considering this has happened every time, it's hard to ignore that I'm the common denominator. I am not saying that the issue was only me in each case, but it's concerning.

Might other people have different interpretations of this same situation? What are they?

Maybe? I guess so? The women might have a different interpretation, but asking them would be awkward, and nobody wants to give out that information.

Am I looking at all the evidence, or just what supports my thoughts?

This is hard to address. I don't have all the evidence because 50% of it walked away when the date ended, so I can only go on what's left over at the end of the date. Truthfully, I don't know why the dates didn't work out, and I have to remember there were cases where I didn't pursue additional dates because *I* wasn't interested. I think that's the first time I've remembered that fact.

Could my thought be an exaggeration of what's true?

These questions helped me realize that I was exaggerating at least a little bit. I haven't pursued 50 women for a second date. This is really the first time I acknowledged that I wasn't interested in many ladies.

Am I having this thought out of habit, or do the facts support it?

I don't think the facts support it the way I thought they did. I may have just been really psyched up about the possibility of developing relationships with some women who rejected me. I was way too hasty in my thought process, and when it went nowhere, the rejection was worse than I expected.

Did someone pass this thought/belief to me? If so, are they a reliable source?

No, not really. I was in a long-term relationship with my previous girlfriend for five years, and I enjoyed that. I would like that kind of relationship again, and I've been doing everything I can to rush into that without realizing that maybe this isn't something you can rush.

Is my thought a likely scenario, or is it the worst-case scenario?

My thought is probably a manifestation of my biggest fear, being alone. I've always wanted to settle down and have a family. I don't know if it's a worst-case scenario exactly, but I would say that the more rejections I experienced, the more pressure at dating and finding the right person I felt.

In the above exercise, we can now see Tom identify that while he's had a lot of dates over the past year, he has not tried to pursue them all for second dates. We get much better insight, but most importantly, so does Tom, about why he may be failing in his dating life. Now he can take this exercise back to his therapist, and together they can work collaboratively on strategies to help him be more successful at dating again.

Chapter 5: How to Ask Better Questions as a Leader

How to Effectively Use Socratic Questioning as a Leader

Being a leader is not an easy task. Challenges can increase when leadership changes or leaders attempt to change the culture of their business. This is a paradigm shift for the organization, and acquiring the "buy-in" from the organization's employees can be challenging. Let's suppose an employer wants its employees to step up their performance to meet specific goals. As a reward, employees who meet performance goals will receive monetary bonuses, and the focus of the organization will shift on the staff's performance versus the number of hours they put in at the office.

The organization leaders can announce these changes to their staff in several ways. They can simply make a statement and expect the staff to jump on board or apply Socratic questioning to pump up and excite their employees about the changes. Let's see how that might look.[liv]

Leader: Can our business meet and exceed its sales goals?

Staff: You bet we can.

Leader: If we meet our goals, should we be eligible for bonuses?

Staff: Absolutely.

Leader: What if one of us is efficient and teaches us how to reach our goals with less work, meaning we need not spend as much time in the office?

Staff: That would be awesome!

Leader: Is it just as good as working a full, forty-hour week to achieve the same results?

Staff: Definitely.

Leader: How would we factor that into how bonuses are calculated?

Staff: It should be based on overall performance and reaching sales goals.

In this example, the leader has brought the staff around to a conclusion about how bonuses will be calculated by having them answer pre-planned questions. With that process, the leader has also excited the staff about the possibilities of future bonuses that await them. The staff now feel a part of the decision to restructure the organization's culture over having such a momentous change simply mandated to them.

One of the bigger challenges a leader can face is connecting each employee to the organization's mission and goals. Suppose the purpose behind your organization is to provide lasting homes to stray animals in your area. As the director of this organization, you attend meetings and fundraise to the public explaining the things your organization does to achieve its goals. You work with veterinarians who help assess your animals and make sure they are healthy enough to be adopted, but also spay and neuter them to avoid contributing to pet overpopulation. You work with several people who assess the potential owners to ensure they are good fits for the adoptable animals, so you aren't placing skittish animals in a home with small children or larger animals in a tiny apartment.

But what about those people who come in daily to clean up after the animals? Or help in situations with no hope, and the animal has to be euthanized? How do you explain the mission and goal of your organization to those who may not get to see how their role impacts the bigger picture? As a quality leader, you should be able to see the value of all your employees and help them see the value and need of what they do in your organization. One way you can do this is by asking "how" and "why." [14] Let's use the animal shelter example to address the questions below with an employee who helps keep the cages clean, and the animals walked and fed.

Director: Why do the dog and cat cages need to be cleaned regularly?

Staff: So, the animals can reduce their stress levels, stay healthy, and maintain proper standards of care.

Director: What does having animals that are healthy and less stressed achieve?

Staff: Those animals are ready for adoption, and people who come in to adopt them will see they are healthy and happy.

Director: Why is that important?

Staff: The animals are more likely to be adopted, which opens up space for other animals that may otherwise have to go to another shelter.

Director: Why don't we want animals to go to other shelters?

Staff: The majority of shelters in our
                area euthanize animals due to
                the shortage in the availability
                of space. So, the more animals
                we adopt out to good homes,
                the more space we have for
                others who need it.

Using the Socratic method, this leader helped this employee pinpoint the crucial role they play in the overall functioning of the organization. An employee can rarely take their job description and their company's mission and find how the two align. If you, as a leader, can show them how they play a pivotal role in the organization's success and that they aren't simply pushing paper around a desk, you can connect to your workforce in a way that money cannot. People feel differently about their jobs when they do something they believe in.

How to Make Better Decisions as a Leader?

As a leader, you need to self-assess your thoughts and reasoning. Applying the Socratic method to your thoughts and ideas is rather challenging. Your thoughts fly by so quickly that there's rarely any time to consider them. Pondering questions to examine your thoughts and investigating the truth of your hypothesis, idea, or opinion are useful practices. You can make observations and come to realizations you haven't had yet. Let's see a few life areas where you can ask targeted Socratic questions to improve your thinking:

1. Question your goals and plans.

- What do I really want to achieve here?
- Why do I pursue this goal/plan?
- Are my expectations and my deadlines reasonable?
- Do I have a hidden reason I'm pursuing this goal/plan?
- If yes, how would this goal/plan look like without it?
- Am I true to my values in pursuing this goal/plan?

2. Questions about your problems.

- Do I see my problems with clarity and objectivity?
- Am I framing this question with the desired answer in mind?
- Am I questioning this problem in an unbiased way?

- Am I considerate about the feelings of others and my own when I ask this question?

3. Questions about your thought process.

- What sources support my thoughts?
- Did I ever look up/ do I know any sources that might disprove my thought process?
- Are my sources objective and credible?
- Am I only focused on information that proves my point?
- Am I resistant to looking for resources that may disprove my thought process? Why?
- Do I have a reason tied to avoiding the analysis of contradictory information?

4. Question your assumptions.

- What am I assuming in this situation?
- Do I have reasonable assumptions? If so, why do I think they are reasonable?
- Are my assumptions benefitting me in any way?
- Where are my assumptions coming from? Are they truly mine, or did I take them from someone else?

5. Question your perspective.
- Did I choose my perspective independently, or do I have an agenda behind it?
- Am I interested in hearing others out or do I just want to push through with my agenda and win the debate?
- Why am I reluctant to consider another's perspective?

- Why do I care so much about winning the debate?

6. Question your conclusions.

- Are my conclusions objective and valid or subjective and self-serving?
- What sources helped me conclude this? Are they relevant, objective, and curated?
- Am I reluctant to revise my conclusion? Why?
- If I had to get to a different conclusion, what would be it?

7. Question the consequences of your conclusions.

- Did I ever stop to think about the implications of my conclusions/decisions?
- If yes, do I find these implications desirable? How can I change my conclusion to result in desirable consequences?
- If not, am I avoiding thinking about consequences because I fear I may need to change my conclusions? Why is that prospect scary?[lv]

This self-scrutiny can help anyone, not just those in leading positions. However, for leaders, it's vital to show up as unbiased and as inclusive as they can be. Their decisions affect the entire organization, the people working in them, and the consumers who purchase their products and services. Leaders should encourage the application of the

Socratic Method not only on themselves but also as a part of company culture. Opening learning dialogues is vital in today's business world. Applying the Socratic Method to a company's problem-solving agenda can lead to a more well-rounded and inclusive analysis.

Despite its utility, the Socratic Method is not as widely applied in organizations as it should be. Why? Because it's easier to tell employees what to do than to open a dialogue about their thoughts, experiences, and suggestions related to a problem. This problem management may be quick in the short run, but it may backfire later. When people are not encouraged and taught how to think for themselves, they merely become droids in the company's ecosystem, blindly executing orders, even when there would be better solutions the upper management can't see. Asking questions thus instead of just giving answers can skyrocket creative and critical thinking, innovation, and even employee satisfaction. People like to feel seen, heard, and important.

Did you ever encounter a micro-manager? Or better put, a micromanaging manager? This is an overworked, anxious person in a leading position with strong perfectionistic tendencies who constantly interferes with the work of their subordinates. They give explicit details on how to do even the smallest aspect of the work, remind people of obvious things multiple times a day, require frequent and detailed progress reports. They never sleep, never eat, and despite all this, barely make the required quota at the end of the quarter. Why? Because:

- a.) they don't do their job, they basically do their employee's job;
- b.) their team is stressed, overly focused on creating the perfect work fitting the manager's expectations instead of ever thinking how could this be done differently, faster, or better;
- c.) some employees can't put up with the pressure and quit, creating a higher demand to hire and train new people;
- d.) if the manager falls ill, nobody knows what to do because they were never taught basic skills to individually run the most important tasks of their department.

Micromanaging does no one a favor. It shows a lack of trust in the skills of the employees, which could be a sign of poor hiring. Micromanaging can also signify a big ego sheltering low self-esteem. Luckily, a cure for micromanagement has only been around for 2,000-something years. Yes, you guessed it right – the Socratic Method.

How can you introduce the Socratic Method in your company?

1. Ask for employee opinion

Say you are a middle manager. Your boss told you that in the first and second quarter your division is responsible for increasing customer satisfaction by 15%. This would be measured based on the reviews they write and the number of products they return. Instead of ordering your employees to push harder in persuading customers to write good reviews, you could say, "We need to achieve a 15% increase in customer satisfaction by the end of the second quarter. What do you think, how could we achieve this?"

They will throw out ideas such as being more personable when offering help over the phone, giving them a little extra when they purchase the product, offering bundles, being more vocal about the importance of reviews, etc. Your employees may have insider views that upper management doesn't know about.

2. Try to focus on solutions instead of the problem.

When using Socratic questioning, try to drift the attention of the employees to be solution-oriented instead of problem-oriented. For example, if customers complain about longer than expected customer support response time, instead of just barking "respond within a day" or "why don't you respond quicker?", you can phrase your question the following way, "what do you need to be able to answer customer emails within 24 hours?"

This question can open a learning dialogue where you may realize that your employees are overworked or don't know how to solve the customers' problems. Once you learn your employee's reason behind the delayed response time, you can ask them what it would take to create the best environment for quick responses. Should you hire someone else? Do they need extra training? Allowing your employees to be part of the solution will help them feel more important and be more invested in good future performance.

If, instead, you hold them a 30-minute meeting, preaching about how slow responsiveness creates angry customers and bad reviews, how that's bad for the company, the employee will raise a brow, "so what?" They need to feel like an important part of the company's structure to care about it. If they are reprimanded, treated as work tools, without ever considering the issues they face, employees won't care about anything but their paycheck and Fridays.

3. The Socratic method isn't always the answer.

A good manager knows when to inquire and when to manage. When your employee seeks your council about a problem they are facing and you say, "well, how would you solve this problem?" they will be perplexed. "I don't know. That's why I'm here for, asking YOU," they may think. Employees do need your guidance sometimes to perform their job more efficiently.

The Socratic method works best when multiple people are involved in problem-solving, team projects, and when the manager asks the first (Socratic) question. In one-on-one situations, especially when the employee initiates the inquiry, it's better to avoid the Socratic Method.[lvi]

Using the Socratic Method in problem-solving can take longer than simply telling your employees what to do, but it encourages a more creative, inclusive, and empowering work environment. It also fosters employee loyalty and satisfaction.

Conclusion

I hope you can see yourself using Socratic questioning at work and in your everyday life to help you reach your goals. The Socratic method is a technique you can count on, from trying to define vague concepts that can have many definitions to persuading your boss to see your viewpoint for why you deserve a raise.

Remember that Socrates practiced his philosophy by using simple conversation. It can be harder to persuade someone in your direction if you're beating them over the head with facts and figures and judgments.

Approach situations as if they were a conversation, and don't forget that making assumptions can be helpful if you can justify your thinking.

Thank you for taking the time to read this book and learn the principles. I hope you take the time to seek opportunities to use Socratic questioning and then do so with confidence. Don't worry if you're unsure at first. The more you practice, the more confident you will become. Remember, this isn't an argument or a debate. You need only to have a conversation, just like Socrates.

Best of luck,

Steven

References

A. (2021, February 12). *The Ideas of Socrates*. Academy of Ideas | Free Minds for a Free Society. Retrieved February 4, 2022, from https://academyofideas.com/2013/04/the-ideas-of-socrates/

Barnes-Brown, A. (2018, July 11). *The Oracle of Delphi: How the Ancient Greeks Relied on One Woman's Divine Visions*. All About History. Retrieved February 4, 2022, from https://www.historyanswers.co.uk/ancient/oracle-of-delphi/

BBC. (2020, June). *Golden State Killer pleads guilty to 13 murders*.

Berger, W. (2019). *The Book of Beautiful Questions: The Powerful Questions That Will Help You Decide, Create, Connect, and Lead* (Reprint ed.). Bloomsbury Publishing.

Bradford, A., & Weisberger, M. (2021, December 7). *Deductive reasoning vs. Inductive reasoning*. Livescience.Com. Retrieved February 4, 2022, from https://www.livescience.com/21569-deduction-vs-induction.html

Brock, F. (2019, September 2). *How to Get to Know Yourself in 5 Fool-Proof Steps*. Prolific Living. Retrieved February 4, 2022, from https://www.prolificliving.com/the-greatest-discovery-of-all-getting-to-know-yourself/

categorical imperative. (n.d.). Oxford Reference. Retrieved February 4, 2022, from https://www.oxfordreference.com/view/1 0.1093/oi/authority.20110803095554912

Chester, N. (2016, April 21). *Criminals Explain How They Justified Their Crimes to Themselves*. Vice. Retrieved February 4, 2022, from https://www.vice.com/en/article/gqmz4m/ how-criminals-justify-crimes-psychology-gangsters-uk

Cochran, M. (1997). McDuff likely to take grisly secrets to grave. *Associated Press*.

Cognitive Restructuring: Socratic Questions (Worksheet). (n.d.). Therapist Aid. Retrieved February 4, 2022, from https://www.therapistaid.com/therapy-worksheet/socratic-questioning

Dr. Paul, R., & Dr. Elder, L. (2006). *The Art of Socratic Questioning.* Criticalthinking.Org. Retrieved February 4, 2022, from https://www.criticalthinking.org/files/SocraticQuestioning2006.pdf

Friedberg, R. (1999, January). *Guidelines for the effective use of Socratic dialogue in cognitive therapy.* Researchgate. Retrieved February 4, 2022, from https://www.researchgate.net/profile/Robert_Friedberg/publication/262141556_Guidelines_for_the_effective_use_of_Socratic_dialogue_in_cognitive_therapy/links/53f25a950cf2bc0c40e8780b/Guidelines-for-the-effective-use-of-Socratic-dialogue-in-cognitive-therapy.pdf

Garud, R. (1997, January). *On the distinction between know-how, know-why, and know-*

what. Researchgate.Net. Retrieved

February 4, 2022, from

https://www.researchgate.net/publication/

285475792_On_the_distinction_between_

know-how_know-why_and_know-what

Gill, N. S. (2019, September 17). *What Was the

Charge Against Socrates?* ThoughtCo.

Retrieved February 4, 2022, from

https://www.thoughtco.com/what-was-

the-charge-against-socrates-121060

Goldhill, O. (2018, August 3). *What makes a

murderer? Science says it's in our brains.*

Quartz. Retrieved February 4, 2022, from

https://qz.com/1348203/a-neuroscientist-

who-studies-rage-says-were-all-capable-

of-doing-something-terrible/

Hare, R. D., & Hare, R. D., PhD. (2021). *Without

Conscience: The Disturbing World of the

Psychopaths Among Us(Unabridged ed.). Tantor and Blackstone Publishing.

Kaplan, R. M. (2009). *Medical Murder: Disturbing Cases of Doctors Who Kill.* Allen & Unwin.

Kibin. (2022). *The Definition of Knowledge According to Socrates | Kibin.* Kibin. Retrieved February 4, 2022, from https://www.kibin.com/essay-examples/the-definition-of-knowledge-according-to-socrates-3HgxZkOl

Kortebein, P. (2018, December 24). *Why Do Some Trees Keep Their Leaves Through Winter? | Three Rivers Park District.* Three Rivers Parks. Retrieved February 4, 2022, from https://www.threeriversparks.org/blog/why-do-some-trees-keep-their-leaves-through-winter

Kraut, R. (2020, December 23). *Socrates |
Biography, Philosophy, Method, Death, &
Facts*. Encyclopedia Britannica.
https://www.britannica.com/biography/So
crates

Kreeft, P., & Dougherty, T. (2010). *Socratic
Logic: A Logic Text using Socratic
Method, Platonic Questions, and
Aristotelian Principles, Edition 3.1* (3rd
ed.). St. Augustines Press.

Learn Law Better. (2018, January 25). *Socratic
Method* [Video]. YouTube.
https://www.youtube.com/watch?v=yIbV
1nzOqgM&t=127s

Milano, S. (2018, August 15). *How to use the
Socratic method in the workplace and
avoid micromanaging*. Quill.Com Blog.
Retrieved February 4, 2022, from
https://www.quill.com/blog/workplace-

culture/how-to-use-the-socratic-method-in-the-workplace-and-avoid-micromanaging.html

Nails, D. (2018, February 6). *Socrates (Stanford Encyclopedia of Philosophy)*. Stanford Encyclopedia of Philosophy. Retrieved February 4, 2022, from https://plato.stanford.edu/entries/socrates/

P. & Plato. (2002). *The Republic*. Spark Pub.

Pink, D. (2012, April 12). *How to move people with two irrational questions | Daniel H. Pink*. Daniel H. Pink | The Official Site of Author Daniel Pink. Retrieved February 4, 2022, from https://www.danpink.com/2012/04/how-to-move-people-with-two-irrational-questions/

Questions for a Socratic Dialogue. (n.d.). Courses.Cs.vt.Edu. Retrieved February 4,

2022, from

https://courses.cs.vt.edu/cs2104/Spring14
McQuain/Notes/SocraticQ.pdf

Robbins, S. (2004, January 19). *How Leaders Use Questions*. HBS Working Knowledge. Retrieved February 4, 2022, from https://hbswk.hbs.edu/archive/how-leaders-use-questions

Robbins, S. (2012, August 6). *How to Persuade Effectively*. Quick and Dirty Tips. Retrieved February 4, 2022, from https://www.quickanddirtytips.com/relationships/professional/how-to-persuade-effectively

Stevens, B. K. (2014, February). *A critique of student development theory : in search of a student development model.*University of Massachusetts Amherst. Retrieved February 4, 2022, from

https://scholarworks.umass.edu/cgi/viewc
ontent.cgi?article=5498&context=disserta
tions_1

T. (2022). *The Socratic Way Of Questioning:
How To Use Socrates' Method To
Discover The Truth And Argue Wisely*. M
& M Limitless Online Inc.

Endnotes

---

[i] Nails, D. (2018, February 6). *Socrates (Stanford Encyclopedia of Philosophy)*. Stanford Encyclopedia of Philosophy. Retrieved February 4, 2022, from https://plato.stanford.edu/entries/socrates/

[ii] Nails, D. (2018, February 6). *Socrates (Stanford Encyclopedia of Philosophy)*. Stanford Encyclopedia of Philosophy. Retrieved February 4, 2022, from https://plato.stanford.edu/entries/socrates/

[iii] Nails, D. (2018, February 6). *Socrates (Stanford Encyclopedia of Philosophy)*. Stanford Encyclopedia of Philosophy. Retrieved February 4, 2022, from

https://plato.stanford.edu/entries/socrates/

[iv] Kraut, R. (2020, December 23). *Socrates |
Biography, Philosophy, Method, Death, &
Facts*. Encyclopedia Britannica.
https://www.britannica.com/biography/So
crates

[v] Nails, D. (2018, February 6). *Socrates (Stanford
Encyclopedia of Philosophy)*. Stanford
Encyclopedia of Philosophy. Retrieved
February 4, 2022, from
https://plato.stanford.edu/entries/socrates/

[vi] Kraut, R. (2020, December 23). *Socrates |
Biography, Philosophy, Method, Death, &
Facts*. Encyclopedia Britannica.
https://www.britannica.com/biography/So
crates

[vii] Kraut, R. (2020, December 23). *Socrates |
Biography, Philosophy, Method, Death, &

Facts. Encyclopedia Britannica.

https://www.britannica.com/biography/So

crates

[viii] Kraut, R. (2020, December 23). *Socrates |*

Biography, Philosophy, Method, Death, &

Facts. Encyclopedia Britannica.

https://www.britannica.com/biography/So

crates

[ix] Kraut, R. (2020, December 23). *Socrates |*

Biography, Philosophy, Method, Death, &

Facts. Encyclopedia Britannica.

https://www.britannica.com/biography/So

crates

[x] Nails, D. (2018, February 6). *Socrates (Stanford*

Encyclopedia of Philosophy). Stanford

Encyclopedia of Philosophy. Retrieved

February 4, 2022, from

https://plato.stanford.edu/entries/socrates/

[xi] Barnes-Brown, A. (2018, July 11). *The Oracle of Delphi: How the Ancient Greeks Relied on One Woman's Divine Visions*. All About History. Retrieved February 4, 2022, from https://www.historyanswers.co.uk/ancient /oracle-of-delphi/

[xii] *Cognitive Restructuring: Socratic Questions (Worksheet)*. (n.d.). Therapist Aid. Retrieved February 4, 2022, from https://www.therapistaid.com/therapy-worksheet/socratic-questioning

[xiii] Cochran, M. (1997). McDuff likely to take grisly secrets to grave. *Associated Press*.

[xiv] Cochran, M. (1997). McDuff likely to take grisly secrets to grave. *Associated Press*.

[xv] P. & Plato. (2002). *The Republic*. Spark Pub.

[xvi] Kibin. (2022). *The Definition of Knowledge*

According to Socrates | Kibin. Kibin.
Retrieved February 4, 2022, from
https://www.kibin.com/essay-
examples/the-definition-of-knowledge-
according-to-socrates-3HgxZkOl

[xvii] Stevens, B. K. (2014, February). *A critique of
student development theory : in search of
a student development model.* University
of Massachusetts Amherst. Retrieved
February 4, 2022, from
https://scholarworks.umass.edu/cgi/viewc
ontent.cgi?article=5498&context=disserta
tions_1

[xviii] Kibin. (2022). *The Definition of Knowledge
According to Socrates | Kibin.* Kibin.
Retrieved February 4, 2022, from
https://www.kibin.com/essay-
examples/the-definition-of-knowledge-

according-to-socrates-3HgxZkO1

[xix] Kreeft, P., & Dougherty, T. (2010). *Socratic Logic: A Logic Text using Socratic Method, Platonic Questions, and Aristotelian Principles, Edition 3.1* (3rd ed.). St. Augustines Press.

[xx] Kreeft, P., & Dougherty, T. (2010). *Socratic Logic: A Logic Text using Socratic Method, Platonic Questions, and Aristotelian Principles, Edition 3.1* (3rd ed.). St. Augustines Press.

[xxi] Bradford, A., & Weisberger, M. (2021, December 7). *Deductive reasoning vs. Inductive reasoning.* Livescience.Com. Retrieved February 4, 2022, from https://www.livescience.com/21569-deduction-vs-induction.html

[xxii] Bradford, A., & Weisberger, M. (2021,

December 7). *Deductive reasoning vs.*

Inductive reasoning. Livescience.Com.

Retrieved February 4, 2022, from

https://www.livescience.com/21569-

deduction-vs-induction.html

[xxiii] https://www.uis.edu/ion/resources/instructional-activities-index/inductive-reasoning/

[xxiv] Bradford, A., & Weisberger, M. (2021,

December 7). *Deductive reasoning vs.*

Inductive reasoning. Livescience.Com.

Retrieved February 4, 2022, from

https://www.livescience.com/21569-

deduction-vs-induction.html

[xxv] Dr. Paul, R., & Dr. Elder, L. (2006). *The Art*

of Socratic Questioning.

Criticalthinking.Org. Retrieved February

4, 2022, from

https://www.criticalthinking.org/files/Socr

aticQuestioning2006.pdf

[xxvi] Dr. Paul, R., & Dr. Elder, L. (2006). *The Art of Socratic Questioning.* Criticalthinking.Org. Retrieved February 4, 2022, from https://www.criticalthinking.org/files/Socr aticQuestioning2006.pdf

[xxvii] Dr. Paul, R., & Dr. Elder, L. (2006). *The Art of Socratic Questioning.* Criticalthinking.Org. Retrieved February 4, 2022, from https://www.criticalthinking.org/files/Socr aticQuestioning2006.pdf

[xxviii] *Questions for a Socratic Dialogue.* (n.d.). Courses.Cs.vt.Edu. Retrieved February 4, 2022, from https://courses.cs.vt.edu/cs2104/Spring14 McQuain/Notes/SocraticQ.pdf

[xxix] Berger, W. (2019). *The Book of Beautiful Questions: The Powerful Questions That Will Help You Decide, Create, Connect, and Lead* (Reprint ed.). Bloomsbury Publishing.

[xxx] *categorical imperative*. (n.d.). Oxford Reference. Retrieved February 4, 2022, from https://www.oxfordreference.com/view/1 0.1093/oi/authority.20110803095554912

[xxxi] Kraut, R. (2020, December 23). *Socrates | Biography, Philosophy, Method, Death, & Facts*. Encyclopedia Britannica. https://www.britannica.com/biography/So crates

[xxxii] A. (2021, February 12). *The Ideas of Socrates*. Academy of Ideas | Free Minds for a Free Society. Retrieved February 4,

2022, from
https://academyofideas.com/2013/04/the-ideas-of-socrates/

xxxiii Goldhill, O. (2018, August 3). *What makes a murderer? Science says it's in our brains.* Quartz. Retrieved February 4, 2022, from https://qz.com/1348203/a-neuroscientist-who-studies-rage-says-were-all-capable-of-doing-something-terrible/

xxxiv Goldhill, O. (2018, August 3). *What makes a murderer? Science says it's in our brains.* Quartz. Retrieved February 4, 2022, from https://qz.com/1348203/a-neuroscientist-who-studies-rage-says-were-all-capable-of-doing-something-terrible/

xxxv Chester, N. (2016, April 21). *Criminals Explain How They Justified Their Crimes to Themselves.* Vice. Retrieved February

4, 2022, from

https://www.vice.com/en/article/gqmz4m/
how-criminals-justify-crimes-psychology-
gangsters-uk

xxxvi Brock, F. (2019, September 2). *How to Get
to Know Yourself in 5 Fool-Proof Steps.*
Prolific Living. Retrieved February 4,
2022, from
https://www.prolificliving.com/the-
greatest-discovery-of-all-getting-to-know-
yourself/

xxxvii Learn Law Better. (2018, January
25). *Socratic Method* [Video]. YouTube.
https://www.youtube.com/watch?v=yIbV
1nzOqgM&t=127s

xxxviii Gill, N. S. (2019, September 17). *What Was
the Charge Against Socrates?* ThoughtCo.
Retrieved February 4, 2022, from

https://www.thoughtco.com/what-was-the-charge-against-socrates-121060

xxxix BBC. (2020, June). *Golden State Killer pleads guilty to 13 murders.* Retrived February 4, 2022.

xl Hare, R. D., & Hare, R. D., PhD. (2021). *Without Conscience: The Disturbing World of the Psychopaths Among Us* (Unabridged ed.). Tantor and Blackstone Publishing. Pg.23.

xli Kaplan, R. M. (2009). *Medical Murder: Disturbing Cases of Doctors Who Kill.* Allen & Unwin.

xlii Robbins, S. (2012, August 6). *How to Persuade Effectively.* Quick and Dirty Tips. Retrieved February 4, 2022, from https://www.quickanddirtytips.com/relationships/professional/how-to-persuade-effectively

[xliii] Robbins, S. (2012, August 6). *How to Persuade Effectively*. Quick and Dirty Tips. Retrieved February 4, 2022, from https://www.quickanddirtytips.com/relationships/professional/how-to-persuade-effectively

[xliv] Robbins, S. (2012, August 6). *How to Persuade Effectively*. Quick and Dirty Tips. Retrieved February 4, 2022, from https://www.quickanddirtytips.com/relationships/professional/how-to-persuade-effectively

[xlv] Pink, D. (2012, April 12). *How to move people with two irrational questions | Daniel H. Pink*. Daniel H. Pink | The Official Site of Author Daniel Pink. Retrieved February 4, 2022, from

https://www.danpink.com/2012/04/how-to-move-people-with-two-irrational-questions/

[xlvi] Pink, D. (2012, April 12). *How to move people with two irrational questions | Daniel H. Pink.* Daniel H. Pink | The Official Site of Author Daniel Pink. Retrieved February 4, 2022, from https://www.danpink.com/2012/04/how-to-move-people-with-two-irrational-questions/

[xlvii] Garud, R. (1997, January). *On the distinction between know-how, know-why, and know-what.* Researchgate.Net. Retrieved February 4, 2022, from https://www.researchgate.net/publication/285475792_On_the_distinction_between_know-how_know-why_and_know-what

xlviii Kortebein, P. (2018, December 24). *Why Do Some Trees Keep Their Leaves Through Winter? | Three Rivers Park District.* Three Rivers Parks. Retrieved February 4, 2022, from https://www.threeriversparks.org/blog/why-do-some-trees-keep-their-leaves-through-winter

xlix Robbins, S. (2012, August 6). *How to Persuade Effectively.* Quick and Dirty Tips. Retrieved February 4, 2022, from https://www.quickanddirtytips.com/relationships/professional/how-to-persuade-effectively

l *Cognitive Restructuring: Socratic Questions (Worksheet).* (n.d.). Therapist Aid. Retrieved February 4, 2022, from https://www.therapistaid.com/therapy-worksheet/socratic-questioning

[li]Friedberg, R. (1999, January). *Guidelines for the effective use of Socratic dialogue in cognitive therapy*. Researchgate. Retrieved February 4, 2022, from https://www.researchgate.net/profile/Robe rt_Friedberg/publication/262141556_Gui delines_for_the_effective_use_of_Socrati c_dialogue_in_cognitive_therapy/links/53 f25a950cf2bc0c40e8780b/Guidelines-for-the-effective-use-of-Socratic-dialogue-in-cognitive-therapy.pdf

[lii]Friedberg, R. (1999, January). *Guidelines for the effective use of Socratic dialogue in cognitive therapy*. Researchgate. Retrieved February 4, 2022, from https://www.researchgate.net/profile/Robe rt_Friedberg/publication/262141556_Gui

delines_for_the_effective_use_of_Socrati

c_dialogue_in_cognitive_therapy/links/53

f25a950cf2bc0c40e8780b/Guidelines-for-

the-effective-use-of-Socratic-dialogue-in-

cognitive-therapy.pdf

[liii] *Cognitive Restructuring: Socratic Questions (Worksheet).* (n.d.). Therapist Aid. Retrieved February 4, 2022, from https://www.therapistaid.com/therapy-worksheet/socratic-questioning

[liv] Robbins, S. (2004, January 19). *How Leaders Use Questions.* HBS Working Knowledge. Retrieved February 4, 2022, from https://hbswk.hbs.edu/archive/how-leaders-use-questions

[lv] T. (2022). *The Socratic Way Of Questioning: How To Use Socrates' Method To Discover The Truth And Argue Wisely.* M

& M Limitless Online Inc.

[lvi] Milano, S. (2018, August 15). *How to use the Socratic method in the workplace and avoid micromanaging.* Quill.Com Blog. Retrieved February 4, 2022, from https://www.quill.com/blog/workplace-culture/how-to-use-the-socratic-method-in-the-workplace-and-avoid-micromanaging.html

Made in the USA
Middletown, DE
02 August 2024